ID667164

X

Elizabethan·Songs

Elizabethan · Songs "in · Honour · of Love · and · Beautie"

Collected · and · Illustrated · by
Edmund · H · Garrett
with · an · introduction · by
Andrew · Lang

Granger Index Reprint Series

BOOKS FOR LIBRARIES PRESS
FREEPORT, NEW YORK

First Published 1891
Reprinted 1970

STANDARD BOOK NUMBER:
8369-6144-7

LIBRARY OF CONGRESS CATALOG CARD NUMBER:
74-116403

MANUFACTURED
BY
HALLMARK LITHOGRAPHERS, INC.
IN THE U.S.A.

"Thus we salute thee with our early song,
And welcome thee and wish thee long."

MILTON.

Contents·

*I had rather than forty shillings I had my book of
songs and sonnets here.*

MERRY WIVES OF WINDSOR.

vii

Elizabethan Songs.

Contents.

Contents.

Elizabethan Songs.

An Index
to
First Lines

*They were old-fashioned poetry, but
choicely good.*

IZAAC WALTON.

xiii

Elizabethan Songs.

Index to First Lines.

Elizabethan Songs.

LIST OF ILLUSTRATIONS

Dost thou love pictures?

TAMING OF THE SHREW.

The illustrations, reproduced by photogravure, are from water-color drawings. Six of them, decorative and emblematic figures, are printed in sepia. They represent six characters, — Grace, Love, Harmony, Revel, Sport, and Laughter, — from a masque by Ben Jonson, written for a Christmas revel at the Court of JAMES I. in 1617. The fifty headings and tail-pieces are from pen-and-ink drawings.

xvii

List of Illustrations.

Here follows prose.

TWELFTH NIGHT.

WHY was the Elizabethan Age, and why were the ages that succeeded Elizabeth, down to the Restoration, so rich in song; and why have later periods been so poor? In this volume of selected verse the word "Elizabethan" is used in a wide sense: we come down as far as Waller, who died in 1686, and Herrick, who died in 1674. The songs of the writers from Shakespeare to Waller sing themselves, as we may say they have their own natural music, and like Philomel in Homer pour forth their

---

turns and trills upon the night; but since that melodious century, the songs of our poets do not sing themselves, as a rule. They are musical, indeed; but somehow they are not easily wedded to music, and the songs which we hear sung are seldom poetry. There are, of course, exceptions. Among these the songs of Burns can hardly be reckoned perhaps as helpful in answering our question, because Burns deliberately and assiduously adapted his words to Scottish airs then already in existence. The good old Scottish tunes went with old words often coarse, perhaps yet more often foolish and almost senseless; Burns supplied new and beautiful language and passion, but the singing quality was present already in the ancient music. Scott's songs, again, were often made to music, as in the case of " Bonny Dundee." Others which he wrote, like "Proud Maisie," are as admirable as any which are handed down from the age of song; but who sings them?

The Scottish poets, like Lady Nairne, gave us immortal songs; but the music was either old, or the singer was his own, or her own, composer.

Our lack of songs is not due to lack of poets. Lord Tennyson, Shelley, and Swinburne have written verse as musical as any that the English language can boast of; and as much may be said for Edgar Poe. But any ear can discern that the new harmonies are different from the Elizabethan harmonies, — are more formal, perhaps, certainly less like birds' notes; that the cadences are more expected, less happily surprising. The songs of these poets are not favorites with musicians; Shelley in particular is rarely sung. Meanwhile such versifiers as Thomas Haynes Bayly have been highly popular with singers, and every one admits that most of our popular songs, with the exception of Dibden's and a few others, are, considered as poetry, worthless. The author of "Oh, no, we never mention her," and "She wore a wreath of roses," was himself a musician; and so was Moore, many of whose songs naturally escape the general condemnation. Why things are thus, is perhaps a question to be answered by musicians rather than by lovers of poetry. The divorce between Music and Poetry is pronounced. Most modern poets rather hate music than love it; most popular composers appear to dislike poetry. Of Victor Hugo we are told that he "especially detested the piano." Gautier called music "the most expensive and the least agreeable of noises." Of recent and living English poets, I fear only two have loved music well,— Mr. Browning, and Mr. Robert Bridges. Of these two, nobody would remark Mr. Browning as particularly skilled in verbal melodies; though there is a song in "Paracelsus" which seems to show that Mr. Browning wrote inharmonious verse by choice, and not because melody was beyond his genius.

It seems, therefore, that modern poets, being unmusical, do not produce songs particularly well-suited for singing; while we must assume that the older singers really wrote for the purpose of being sung, and were themselves musicians and lovers of music. Yet even on this head we have

xxii

not always certainty; for poets affect in their verse to like music, even though they secretly share the sentiments of Victor Hugo. Yet our inclination to believe in the true love of music among the Elizabethans is strengthened by the manner of their publication. It is from rare "Books of Airs" that Mr. Bullen has gathered the poems of Campion, and of many others with which he has enriched our poetry. Campion himself wrote much of his own music in "A Book of Airs" (1601). As he himself says, "I have chiefly aimed to couple my words and notes lovingly together." "The lute Orpherian and base violl" seem to have been ever in our ancestors' hands; and the singing humor was thus strong in Walton's day, "when," as the milk-woman says, "Young Coridon played so purely on his pipe to you and your cousin Betty." Not now shall we find milkmaids who know "Come, Shepherds, deck your heads," or "Phillida flouts me," or "Johnny Armstrong," or "Troy Town." Education is hostile to literature. The untaught country folk of Walton's age were familiar with good poetry; the instructed people of to-day sing music-hall trash, if they sing anything. By Test or Kennet no angler shall hear fair Maudlin chant that smooth song which was made by Kit Marlowe, now at least fifty years ago! Utopia is behind us.

The astonishing thing is that in the age of poetry, from 1570 to 1670, all the poets, with hardly an exception, were natural singers. That Shakespeare had this gift is no marvel, when once the miracle of his universality is granted. But Marlowe, and Beaumont and Fletcher, and the ponderously learned Ben Jonson, and the sombre Webster were all song-makers, — all had that lost inimitable art, that unconscious charm. The gift descended even to authors now unknown or unnoted, — to all who were " sealed of the tribe of Ben," like " my son William Cartwright" with his —

> " Hark, my Flora! Love doth call us
> To that strife that must befall us."

It may be said that the tempests of our age have silenced song, as linnets are quiet before

*the storm. But the civil wars did not quench
the music of Suckling and Herrick, of Cartwright
and Carew. Prison and battle only inspire the
muse of Lovelace, as in his —*

> *" If to be absent were to be
>   Away from thee,"*

and this purest chant of spiritual affection, —

> *" Above the highest sphere wee meet
>   Unseene, unknowne, and greet as angels greet."*

*Still his mind is full of love and beauty, as in
" To Amarantha, that she would dishevell her
haire." These songs we learn from Lovelace's
" Lucasta" (1649) were " set" by Mr. Henry
Lawes and Mr. John Laniere and Mr. Hudson
and Dr. John Wilson ; and it was Mr. Thomas
Charles who " set" the gallant impertinence of —*

> *" Why should you swear I am forsworn
>   Since thine I vow'd to be?
> Lady, it is already morn,
>   And 't was last night I swore to thee
>   That fond impossibility."*

*The music and the words, in all that age, were
twins from the birth. I happen to have here*

"*Poems, Songs, and Sonnets, together with a Masque, by Thomas Carew, Esq. The Fourth Edition. London, 1671.*" *Some former owner has written in an old hand on the fly-leaf,* "*The Songs set in Musick in H. Lawes's Ayres and Dialogues for One, Two, and Three Voyces.*"

While music and verse thus lived inseparable, Carew, in an age long after the Elizabethan, could write —

> "*Ask me no more where Jove bestows,*
> *When June is past, the fading Rose,*"

and —

> "*He that loves a rosie cheek*
> *Or a coral lip admires.*"

Herrick says little of music in his "*Hesperides,*" *save to complain that when* —

> "*The bad season makes the Poet sad,*"

he is —

> "*Dull to myself, and almost dead to these*
> *My many fresh and fragrant mistresses,*
> *Lost to all music now.*"

But Herrick, too, retains that Elizabethan lilt, as in the "*Mad Maid's Song,*" —

Introduction.

"*Good-morrow to the day so fair,*
Good-morrow, sir, to you;
Good-morrow to mine own torn hair,
Bedabbled with the dew."

Herrick gratefully addresses " Mr. Henry
Lawes, the Excellent Composer of his Lyrics,"
and while praising him praises also "rare
Laniere," "rare Gotire," and "curious Wilson."
The songs of that century were never written,
as lyrics now have long been written, except
for the purpose of being sung. They were
meant for voices in masques or in plays, inter-
ludes of music in dance or in action; or they
were such nuptial songs and epithalamies as the
manners of frank and joyous people required.
Thus our lyric poetry of that period answered,
in its way, to the lyric poetry of Greece in the
period of Sappho and Alcæus. Unfortunately
for our singers, the bulk of the Greek song of
that date is lost; but they fell back on what
ancient inspirations they had to hand,—and in
the floral verse of Herrick, especially, there are
frequent imitations of the Greek Anthology.

Herrick rejoices in that pleasing confusion of flowers and maids and delights, and despite "his Noble Numbers or his Pious Pieces" is as great a heathen as Paulus Silentiarius. These lyrists are all much inclined to cry, with Campion,—

> "_I care not for these ladies_
> _That must be vowed and prayed;_
> _Give me kind Amaryllis,_
> _The wanton country maid._"

Their happy and unreflecting wantonness makes, no doubt, part of their charm; and this, it may be said, was nearly killed by Puritanism, was only blown into a brief aud hectic flame by the orgy of the Restoration, and quite expired, even in Dryden's songs, under non-lyrical French influences. The last echoes of Elizabethan melody fade away in some of the latest love-songs in Mr. Bullen's "Love Poems from the Song-Books of the Seventeenth Century," as in the epithalamium from "Wit at a Venture" (1674), written by Robert Barns (1650),—

Introduction.

> "Be young to each when winter and gray hairs
>   Your head shall climb;
> May your affections like the merry spheres
>   Still move in time,
> And may (with many a good presage)
>   Your marriage prove your merry age."

Changed times, changed minds! "Marriage is a failure!" and who calls the spheres merry? "Weary" is a likelier epithet. Mr. Carlyle called them "a sad sicht." We must be merry again before we can be musical, save in an erudite, tuneless fashion; and Heaven only knows when we shall be merry again!

We cannot revive that pleasant, careless babble which in some of Shakespeare's songs breaks down into a mirthful nonsense of chorus. We cannot regain that country contentment, that spontaneous melody, which all the singers of a century possess, even as all the dramatists, however worthless, had, as Scott remarks, something great in their style. Education, which was to give us so much, only makes us wonder at the untutored excellence of the common taste in Elizabeth's time, that had to be addressed in language *of a lofty pitch at the play, and that even in tavern-catches demanded and received something exquisite, strange, and not to be renewed, till we renew the freshness of life and the joy of it. The young English Muse is like Sir Edward Dyer's " Phillis, the Fair Shepherdess," —*

> *" My Phillis hath the morning sun*
> *At first to look upon her;*
> *And Phillis hath morn-waking birds*
> *Her rising still to honor."*

But now the English Muse may sing with Gascoigne, —

> *" First, lullaby my youthful years,*
> *It is now time to go to bed;*
> *For crooked age and hoary hairs*
> *Have now their haven within my head.*
> *With lullaby then youth be still,*
> *With lullaby content thy will,*
> *Since courage quails and comes behind;*
> *Go, sleep, and so beguile thy mind."*

The revolving years will bring back again, some day, a world that is glad and clean, and not over-thronged and not overdriven. Some later generation will awake when, as Mr. Bridges sings, —

xxx

Introduction.

"*The merry elves and fairies*
   Are in the woods again,
And play their mad vagaries
   And wanton freaks amain.
'*Come out, come out, good mortals, come!*'
      they cry, 'and share
Our pleasures rare!'
And I that love gay June
Am out ere morn has driven
Her loitering star from heaven,
Or woke the first bird's tune."

Then we shall have courtly singers, like Love-lace and Raleigh, and country pleasures of pipe and tabor. Then England shall not be under a pall of smoke; the bass viol and the lute and the virginals shall be musical, — but the jingle of the piano shall not be heard in the land, and there shall be no hurdy-gurdies any more forever. Meanwhile, we "have our book of songs and sonnets here."

ANDREW LANG.

1, MARLOES ROAD,
   LONDON.

Elizabethan · Songs

"flaunt·they·in·phrases·fine,
Enam'ling·with·pied·flowers·their·thoughts
of gold."

THE·DEFENCE·OF·POESIE

JOHN HARYNGTON.

1534-1582.

A HEART OF STONE.

WHENCE comes my love? O heart, disclose!
   'T was from cheeks that shame the rose;
From lips that spoil the ruby's praise;
From eyes that mock the diamond's blaze.
     Whence comes my love? As freely own:
     Ah, me! 'T was from a heart of stone.

The blushing cheek speaks modest mind;
The lips, befitting words most kind;
The eye does tempt to love's desire,
And seems to say 't is Cupid's fire:
     Yet all so fair but speak my moan,
     Sith nought doth say the heart of stone.

3

Why thus, my love, so kind bespeak
Sweet lip, sweet eyes, sweet blushing cheek,
Yet not a heart to save my pain?
O Venus! take thy gifts again!
     Make not so fair to cause our moan,
     Or make a heart that 's like your own!

GEORGE GASCOIGNE.

1537-1577.

LULLABY OF A LOVER.

SING lullaby, as women do
    Wherewith they bring their babes to rest;
And lullaby can I sing too,
    As womanly as can the best.
With lullaby they still the child;
And if I be not much beguiled,
Full many wanton babes have I
Which must be stilled with lullaby.

First, lullaby my youthful years;
    It is now time to go to bed,
For crooked age and hoary hairs
    Have now the haven within my head.

With lullaby then youth be still,
With lullaby content thy will,
Since courage quails, and comes behind;
Go, sleep! and so beguile thy mind.

Next, lullaby my gazing eyes,
    Which wonted were to glance apace,
For every glass may now suffice
    To show the furrows in my face.
With lullaby then wink a while,
With lullaby your looks beguile;
Let no fair face, nor beauty bright,
Entice you eft with vain delight.

And lullaby my wanton will,
    Let reason's rule now reign my thought,
Since all too late I find by skill
How dear I have thy fancies bought.
With lullaby now take thine ease,
With lullaby thy doubts appease;
For trust to this, — if thou be still,
My body shall obey thy will.

George Gascoigne.

A STRANGE PASSION OF A LOVER.

A MID my bale I bathe in bliss,
  I swim in heaven, I sink in hell:
I find amends for every miss,
  And yet my moan no tongue can tell.
I live and love (what would you more?)
As never lover lived before.

I laugh sometimes with little lust,
  So jest I oft and feel no joy;
Mine eye is builded all on trust,
  And yet mistrust breeds mine annoy.
I live and lack, I lack and have;
I have and miss the thing I crave.

These things seem strange, yet are they true.
  Believe me, sweet, my state is such,
One pleasure which I would eschew
  Both slakes my grief and breeds my grutch;
So doth one pain which I would shun
  Renew my joys where grief begun.

Then like the lark that passed the night
    In heavy sleep with cares oppressed,
Yet when she spies the pleasant light
    She sends sweet notes from out her breast.
So sing I now because I think
How joys approach, when sorrows shrink.

And as fair Philomene again
    Can watch and sing when others sleep,
And taketh pleasure in her pain
    To wray the woe that makes her weep:
So sing I now for to bewray
    The loathsome life I lead alway.

The which to thee, dear wench, I write,
    Thou know'st my mirth but not my moan:
I pray God grant thee deep delight,
    To live in joys when I am gone.
I cannot live; it will not be:
I die to think to part from thee.

SIR EDWARD DYER.

1550-1607.

TO PHILLIS THE FAIR SHEPHERDESS.

MY Phillis hath the morning Sun
　　At first to look upon her:
And Phillis hath morn-waking birds
　　Her rising still to honour.
My Phillis hath prime feathered flowers,
　　That smile when she treads on them:
And Phillis hath a gallant flock
　　That leaps since she doth own them.
But Phillis hath too hard a heart,
　　Alas, that she should have it!
It yields no mercy to desert,
　　Nor grace to those that crave it.

9

Sweet Sun, when thou look'st on,
    Pray her regard my moan !
Sweet birds, when you sing to her,
    To yield some pity woo her !
Sweet flowers that she treads on,
    Tell her her beauty dreads one.
And if in life her love she nill agree me,
Pray her before I die she will come see me.

JOHN LYLY.

1554-1600

DAPHNE.

MY Daphne's hair is twisted gold,
   Bright stars a-piece her eyes do hold;
My Daphne's brow enthrones the graces,
My Daphne's beauty stains all faces;
On Daphne's cheek grow rose and cherry,
On Daphne's lip a sweeter berry;
Daphne's snowy hand but touched does melt,
And then no heavenlier warmth is felt.
My Daphne's voice tunes all the spheres,
My Daphne's music charms all ears;
Fond am I thus to sing her praise,
These glories now are turned to bays.

11

SYRINX.

PAN'S Syrinx was a girl indeed,
   Though now she 's turned into a reed ;
From that dear reed Pan's pipe does come,
A pipe that strikes Apollo dumb.
Nor flute, nor lute, nor gittern can
So chant it as the pipe of Pan ;
Cross-gartered swains and dairy girls,
With faces smug and round as pearls,
When Pan's shrill pipe begins to play,
With dancing wear out night and day ;
The bagpipe's drone his hum lays by,
When Pan sounds up his minstrelsy.
His minstrelsy ! Oh, base ! this quill,
Which at my mouth with wind I fill,
Puts me in mind, though her I miss,
That still my Syrinx's lips I kiss.

John Lyly.

SONG TO APOLLO.

SING to Apollo, god of day,
    Whose golden beams with morning play,
And make her eyes so brightly shine,
Aurora's face is called divine !
Sing to Phœbus and that throne
Of diamonds which he sits upon.
        Io, pæans let us sing
           To Physic's and to Poesy's king !

Crown all his altars with bright fire,
Laurels bind about his lyre,
A Daphnean coronet for his head,
The Muses dance about his bed !
When on his ravishing lute he plays,
Strew his temple round with bays !
        Io, pæans let us sing
           To the glittering Delian king !

LOVE'S COLLEGE.

O CUPID! monarch over kings,
 Wherefore hast thou feet and wings?
It is to show how swift thou art
When thou woundest a tender heart!
Thy wings being clipped, and feet held still,
Thy bow so many could not kill.

It is all one in Venus' wanton school
Who highest sits, the wise man or the fool.
 Fools in love's college
 Have far more knowledge
 To read a woman over,
 Than a neat prating lover:
  Nay, 't is confessed
  That fools please women best.

John Lyly.

SPRING'S WELCOME.

WHAT bird so sings, yet so does wail?
　　Oh 't is the ravished nightingale.
"Jug, jug, jug, jug, tereu," she cries,
And still her woes at midnight rise.
Brave prick-song! who is 't now we hear?
None but the lark so shrill and clear;
How at heaven's gates she claps her wings,
The morn not waking till she sings.
Hark, hark, with what a pretty throat
Poor robin redbreast tunes his note;
Hark, how the jolly cuckoos sing, —
Cuckoo to welcome in the spring!
Cuckoo to welcome in the spring!

CUPID AND CAMPASPE.

CUPID and my Campaspe played
    At cards for kisses : Cupid paid.
He stakes his quiver, bow, and arrows,
His mother's doves, and team of sparrows :
Loses them, too.   Then down he throws
The coral of his lip, the rose
Growing on 's cheek (but none knows how) ;
With these, the crystal of his brow.
And then the dimple of his chin :
All these did my Campaspe win.
At last he set her both his eyes :
She won, and Cupid blind did rise.
O Love ! has she done this to thee ?
What shall, alas ! become of me ?

John Lyly.

ARROWS FOR LOVE.

M^Y shag-hair Cyclops, come, let 's ply
  The Lamnion hammers lustily !
      By my wife's sparrows,
      I swear these arrows
      Shall singing fly
      Through many a wanton's eye.
These headed are with golden blisses,
These silver ones feathered with kisses ;
      But this of lead
      Strikes a clown dead,
      When in a dance
      He falls in a trance,
To see his black-browed lass not buss him,
And then whines out for death t' untruss him.
    So ! so ! our work being done, let 's play.
    Holiday ! boys, cry holiday !

CUPID ARRAIGNED.

FROM "GALATEA."

OH, YES! Oh, yes! if any maid
    Whom leering Cupid has betrayed
To frowns of spite, to eyes of scorn;
And would in madness now see torn
The boy in pieces, — let her come
Hither, and lay on him her doom.

Oh, yes! Oh, yes! has any lost
A heart, which many a sigh hath cost?
Is any cozened of a tear,
Which as a pearl disdain does wear?
Here stands the thief! — let her but come
Hither, and lay on him her doom.

Is any one undone by fire,
And turned to ashes through desire?

Did ever any lady weep,
Being cheated of her golden sleep,
Stol'n by sick thoughts? — the pirate 's found,
And in **her** tears he shall be drowned.

Read his indictment, let him hear
What he 's to trust to. Boy, give ear!

FULKE GREVILLE (Lord Brooke).

1554?-1638.

MYRA.

I WITH whose colors Myra drest her head,
  I that ware posies of her own hand-making,
I that mine own name in the chimnies read,
    By Myra finely wrought ere I was waking:
      Must I look on, in hope time coming may
      With change bring back my turn again to
      play?

I that on Sunday at the church-stile found
  A garland sweet with true-love-knots in flowers,
Which I to wear about mine arms was bound,
  That each of us might know that all was ours:

Fulke Greville.

Must I now lead an idle life in wishes,
And follow Cupid for his loaves and fishes?

I that did wear the ring her mother left,
   I for whose love she gloried to be blamed,
I with whose eyes her eyes committed theft,
   I who did make her blush when I was named:
     Must I lose ring, flowers, blush, theft, and
       go naked,
     Watching with sighs till dead love be awakèd.

TO HER EYES.

YOU little stars that live in skies,
    And glory in Apollo's glory;
In whose aspect conjoinèd lies
    The heaven's will and nature's story, —
Joy to be likened to those eyes,
    Which eyes make all eyes glad or sorry:
        For when you force thoughts from above,
        These overrule your force by love.

And thou, O Love, which in these eyes
    Hast married reason with affection,
And made them saints of beautie's skyes,
    Where joys are shadows of perfection, —
Lend me thy wings that I may rise
    Up, not by worth, but thy election:
        For I have vowed in strangest fashion
        To love, and never seek compassion.

SIR PHILIP SIDNEY.

1554–1586.

ABSENCE.

O DEAR life when shall it be
　　That mine eyes thine eyes shall see,
And in them thy mind discover
Whether absence have had force
Thy remembrance to divorce
From the image of thy lover?

Or if I myself find not,
After parting, aught forgot
Nor debarred from Beauty's treasure,
Let not tongue aspire to tell
In what high joys I shall dwell :
Only thought aims at the pleasure.

23

Thought, therefore I will send thee
To take up the place for me :
Long I will not after tarry ;
There, unseen, thou mayst be bold
Those fair wonders to behold,
Which in them my hopes do carry.

Thought, see thou no place forbear ;
Enter bravely everywhere,
Seize on all to her belonging !
But if thou wouldst guarded be,
Fearing her beams, take with thee
Strength of liking, rage of longing.

Think of that most grateful time,
When my leaping heart will climb
In my lips to have his biding,
There those roses for to kiss
Which do breathe a sugared bliss,
Opening rubies, pearls dividing.

.   .   .   .   .

Think, think of those dallyings,
When with dove-like murmurings,
With glad moaning, passèd anguish,
We change eyes, and heart for heart,
Each to other do depart,
Joying till joy makes us languish.

O my thought! my thoughts surcease,
Thy delights my woes increase,
My life melts with too much thinking!
Think no more, but die in me,
Till thou shalt revivèd be,
At her lips my nectar drinking.

NICHOLAS BRETON.

PHILLIDA AND CORYDON.

IN the merry month of May,
  In a morn by break of day,
Forth I walked by the wood-side,
When as May was in his pride:
There I spièd all alone
Phillida and Corydon.
Much ado there was, God wot;
He would love and she would not.
She said, "Never man was true;"
He said, "None was false to you."
He said he had loved her long;
She said, Love should have no wrong.

Corydon would kiss her then;
She said, Maids must kiss no men
Till they did for good and all.
Then she made the shepherd call
All the heavens to witness truth
Never loved a truer youth.
Thus with many a pretty oath,
Yea and nay, and faith and troth,
Such as silly shepherds use
When they still will love abuse, —
Love, which had been long deluded,
Was with kisses sweet concluded;
And Phillida, with garlands gay,
Was made the lady of the May.

THOMAS LODGE.

1556-1625.

ROSALIND'S MADRIGAL.

LOVE in my bosom like a bee
　　Doth suck his sweet;
Now with his wings he plays with me,
　　Now with his feet.
Within mine eyes he makes his nest;
His bed, amidst my tender breast;
My kisses are his daily feast;
And yet he robs me of my rest, —
　　　　Ah! wanton, will ye?

And if I sleep, then percheth he
　　With pretty flight,
And makes his pillow of my knee
　　The livelong night.

Strike I my lute, he tunes the string;
He music plays, if so I sing;
He lends me every lovely thing;
Yet cruel he, my heart doth sting, —
    Whist, wanton, still ye!

Else I with roses every day
    Will whip you hence;
And bind you, when you long to play,
    For your offence.
I 'll shut mine eyes to keep you in,
I 'll make you fast it for your sin,
I 'll count your power not worth a pin, —
Alas! what hereby shall I win,
    If he gainsay me?

What if I beat the wanton boy
    With many a rod?
He will repay me with annoy,
    Because a god.

Then sit thou safely on my knee,
And let thy bower my bosom be;
Lurk in mine eyes, I like of thee;
O Cupid, so thou pity me,
    Spare not, but play thee.

THE DECEITFUL MISTRESS.

NOW I find thy looks were feignèd,
   Quickly lost, and quickly gainèd;
Soft thy skin like wool of weathers,
Heart unstable, light as feathers,
Tongue untrusty, subtle-sighted,
Wanton will, with change delighted.
     Siren pleasant, foe to reason,
     Cupid plague thee for this treason!

Of thine eyes I made my mirror,
From thy beauty came mine error;
All thy words I counted witty,
All thy smiles I deemèd pity;
Thy false tears, that me aggrievèd,
First of all my heart deceivèd.
     Siren pleasant, foe to reason,
     Cupid plague thee for this treason!

Feigned acceptance, when I asked;
Lovely words, with cunning masked;
Holy vows, but heart unholy;
Wretched man! my trust was folly!

Lily-white, and pretty winking;
Solemn vows, but sorry thinking.
    Siren pleasant, foe to reason,
    Cupid plague thee for this treason!

Now I see, Oh, seemly cruel,
Oh, thus warm them at my fuel,
Wit shall guide me in this durance,
Since in love is no assurance;
Change thy pasture, take thy pleasure,
Beauty is a fading treasure.
    Siren pleasant, foe to reason,
    Cupid plague thee for thy treason!

Prime youth lasts not, age will follow,
And make white those tresses yellow;
Wrinkled face, for looks delightful,
Shall acquaint thee, dame despiteful!
And when time shall date thy glory,
Then, too late, thou wilt be sorry.
    Siren pleasant, foe to reason,
    Cupid plague thee for this treason!

Thomas Lodge.

ROSALIND'S DESCRIPTION.

LIKE to the clear in highest sphere,
　　Where all imperial glory shines,
Of self-same color is her hair,
　　Whether unfolded or in twines :
　　　　Heigho, fair Rosalind !

Her eyes are sapphires set in snow,
　　Refining heaven by every wink ;
The gods do fear when as they glow,
　　And I do tremble when I think :
　　　　Heigho, would she were mine !

Her cheeks are like the blushing cloud
　　That beautifies Aurora's face,
Or like the silver, crimson shroud
　　That Phœbe's smiling looks doth grace :
　　　　Heigho, fair Rosalind !

Her lips are like two budded roses,
  Whom ranks of lilies neighbor nigh,
Within which bounds she balm incloses
  Apt to entice a deity:
    Heigho, would she were mine!

Her neck like to a stately tower,
  Where Love himself imprisoned lies,
To watch for glances every hour,
  From her divine and sacred eyes:
    Heigho, fair Rosalind!

Her paps are centres of delight,
  Her breasts are orbs of heavenly frame,
Where Nature moulds the dew of light,
  To feed Perfection with the same:
    Heigho, would she were mine!

With orient pearl, with ruby red,
  With marble white, with sapphire blue,
Her body every way is fed,
  Yet soft in touch and sweet in' view:
    Heigho, fair Rosalind!

34

Nature herself her shape admires,
    The gods are wounded in her sight,
And Love forsakes his heavenly fires
      And at her eyes his brand doth light :
          Heigho, would she were mine !

Then muse not, nymphs, though I bemoan
    The absence of fair Rosalind,
Since for her fair there is fairer none ;
      Nor for her virtues so divine ;
          Heigho, fair Rosalind !
Heigho, my heart, would God that she were
    mine !

SPRING AND MELANCHOLY.

THE earth, late choked with showers,
   Is now arrayed in green;
Her bosom springs with flowers,
   The air dissolves her teen;
      The heavens laugh at her glory:
      Yet bide I sad and sorry.

The woods are decked with leaves,
   And trees are clothèd gay;
And Flora crowned with sheaves
   With oaken boughs doth play,
      Where I am clad in black
      In token of my wrack.

The birds upon the trees
   Do sing with pleasant voices,
And chant in their degrees
   Their loves and lucky choices;
      When I, whilst they are singing,
      With sighs mine arms am wringing.

The thrushes seek the shade,
   And I my fatal grave;
Their flight to heaven is made,
   My walk on earth I have;
      They free, I thrall; they jolly,
      I sad and pensive wholly.

LOVE'S WANTONNESS.

LOVE guides the roses of thy lips,
    And flies about them like a bee;
If I approach, he forward skips,
    And if I kiss, he stingeth me.

Love in thine eyes doth build his bower,
    And sleeps within their pretty shine;
And if I look the boy will lower,
    And from their orbs shoot shafts divine.

Love works thy heart within his fire,
    And in my tears doth firm the same;
And if I tempt it will retire,
    And of my plaints doth make a game.

Love, let me cull her choicest flowers,
    And pity me, and calm her eye;
Make soft her heart, dissolve her lowers.
    Then I will praise thy deity.

DO ME RIGHT, AND DO ME REASON.

FROM "A LOOKING-GLASS FOR LONDON AND ENGLAND."

BEAUTY, alas! where wast thou born,
   Thus to hold thyself in scorn?
Whenas Beauty kissed to woo thee.
Thou by Beauty dost undo me:
      Heigh-ho! despise me not.

I and thou in sooth are one,—
Fairer thou, I fairer none;
Wanton thou, and wilt thou, wanton,
Yield a cruel heart to plant on?
Do me right, and do me reason;
Cruelty is cursèd treason:
      Heigh-ho! I love.   Heigh-ho! I love.
      Heigh-ho! and yet he eyes me not.

ROBERT GREENE.

1560 ?–1592.

MENAPHON'S SONG.

SOME say Love,
  Foolish Love,
     Doth rule and govern all the gods;
I say Love,
Inconstant Love,
     Sets men's senses far at odds.
Some swear Love,
Smoothed-faced Love,
     Is sweetest sweet that man can have;
I say Love,
Sour Love,
     Makes virtue yield as beauty's slave.
A bitter sweet, a folly worst of all,
That forceth wisdom to be folly's thrall.

Love is sweet!
Wherein sweet?
  In fading pleasures that do pain.
Beauty sweet!
Is that sweet
  That yieldeth sorrow for a gain?
If Love 's sweet,
Herein sweet,
  That minutes' joys are monthly woes.
'T is not sweet,
That is sweet,
  Nowhere but where repentance grows.
Then love who list, if beauty be so sour;
Labor for me, Love rest in prince's bower.

THE SHEPHERD'S WIFE'S SONG.

AH, what is love?   It is a pretty thing,
   As sweet unto a shepherd as a king,
          And sweeter, too;
For kings have cares that wait upon a crown,
And cares can make the sweetest love to frown.
          Ah then, ah then,
   If country loves such sweet desires do gain,
   What lady would not love a shepherd swain?

His flocks are folded; he comes home at night,
As merry as a king in his delight,
          And merrier, too;
For kings bethink them what the state require,
Where shepherds, careless, carol by the fire.
          Ah then, ah then,
   If country loves such sweet desires do gain,
   What lady would not love a shepherd swain?

He kisseth first, then sits as blithe to eat
His cream and curds, as doth the king his meat,
   And blither, too;
For kings have often fears when they do sup,
Where shepherds dread no poison in their cup.
   Ah then, ah then,
  If country loves such sweet desires do gain,
  What lady would not love a shepherd swain?

To bed he goes, as wanton then, I ween,
As is a king in dalliance with a queen;
   More wanton, too, —
For kings have many griefs affects to move,
Where shepherds have no greater grief than love.
   Ah then, ah then,
  If country loves such sweet desires do gain,
  What lady would not love a shepherd swain?

Upon his couch of straw he sleeps as sound
As doth the king upon his beds of down;
   More sounder, too, —
For cares cause kings full oft their sleep to spill,
Where weary shepherds lie and snort their fill.

Ah then, ah then,
If country loves such sweet desires do gain,
What lady would not love a shepherd swain?

Thus, with his wife, he spends the year as blithe
As doth the king at every tide or sithe,
And blither, too;
For kings have wars and broils to take in hand,
Where shepherds laugh and love upon the land.
Ah then, ah then,
Since country loves such sweet desires do gain,
What lady would not love a shepherd swain.

Robert Greene.

CUPID'S INGRATITUDE.

CUPID abroad was 'lated in the night,
　　His wings were wet with ranging in the rain;
Harbor he sought: to me he took his flight
　　To dry his plumes. I heard the boy complain;
I oped the door, and granted his desire;
I rose myself, and made the wag a fire.

Looking more narrow, by the fire's flame,
　　I spied his quiver hanging by his back;
Doubting the boy might my misfortune frame,
　　I would have gone, for fear of further wrack:
But what I dread did me, poor wretch, betide,
For forth he drew an arrow from his side.

He pierced the quick, and I began to start;
　　A pleasing wound, but that it was too high:
His shaft procured a sharp, yet sugared smart.
　　Away he flew; for why, his wings were dry;
But left the arrow sticking in my breast,
That sore I grieved I welcomed such a guest.

INFIDA'S SONG.

SWEET Adon, dar'st not glance thine eye
    N 'oserez vous, mon bel ami?
Upon thy Venus that must die?
    Je vous en prie, pity me;
N 'oserez vous, mon bel, mon bel,
    N 'oserez vous, mon bel ami?

See how sad thy Venus lies,
    N 'oserez vous, mon bel ami?
Love in heart, and tears in eyes,
    Je vous en prie, pity me;
N 'oserez vous, mon bel, mon bel,
    N 'oserez vous, mon bel ami?

Thy face is fair as Paphos' brooks,
    N 'oserez vous, mon bel ami?
Wherein Fancy baits her hooks;
    Je vous en prie, pity me;
N 'oserez vous, mon bel, mon bel,
    N 'oserez vous, mon bel ami?

Thy cheeks like cherries that do grow,
   N 'oserez vous, mon bel ami?
Amongst the western mounts of snow,
   Je vous en prie, pity me;
N 'oserez vous, mon bel, mon bel,
   N 'oserez vous, mon bel ami?

Thy lips vermilion, full of love,
   N 'oserez vous, mon bel ami?
Thy neck as silver-white as dove;
   Je vous en prie, pity me;
N 'oserez vous, mon bel, mon bel,
   N 'oserez vous, mon bel ami?

Thine eyes like flames of holy fires,
   N 'oserez vous, mon bel ami?
Burn all my thoughts with sweet desires;
   Je vous en prie, pity me;
N 'oserez vous, mon bel, mon bel,
   N 'oserez vous, mon bel ami?

All thy beauties sting my heart,
   N 'oserez vous, mon bel ami?

I must die through Cupid's dart;
    Je vous en prie, pity me;
N 'oserez vous, mon bel, mon bel,
    N 'oserez vous, mon bel ami?

Wilt thou let thy Venus die?
    N 'oserez vous, mon bel ami?
Adon were unkind, say I,
    Je vous en prie, pity me;
N 'oserez vous, mon bel, mon bel,
    N 'oserez vous, mon bel ami?

To let fair Venus die for woe,
    N 'oserez vous, mon bel ami?
That doth love sweet Adon so;
    Je vous en prie, pity me;
N 'oserez vous, mon bel, mon bel,
    N 'oserez vous, mon bel ami?

SAMUEL DANIEL.

1562–1619.

LOVE.

LOVE is a sickness full of woes
    All remedies refusing;
A plant that with most cutting grows,
    Most barren with best using.
        Why so?
    More we enjoy it, more it dies;
    If not enjoyed it sighing cries,
        Hey, ho!

Love is a torment of the mind,
    A tempest everlasting;
And Jove hath made it of a kind
    Not well, nor full, nor fasting.
        Why so?
    More we enjoy it, more it dies;
    If not enjoyed it sighing cries,
        Hey, ho!

Samuel Daniel.

A H, I remember well (and how can I
　　But evermore remember well) when first
Our flame began; when scarce we knew what was
The flame we felt; when as we sat and sighed,
And looked upon each other, and conceived
Not what we ail'd, — yet something we did ail;
And yet were well, and yet we were not well;
And what was our disease we could not tell.
Then would we kiss, then sigh, then look: and thus
In that first garden of our simpleness
We spent our childhood.　But when years began
To reap the fruit of knowledge, ah, how then
Would she with graver looks, with sweet stern brow
Check my presumption and my forwardness;
Yet still would give me flowers, still would me show
What she would have me, yet not have me know.

EIDOLA.

ARE they shadows that we see?
    And can shadows pleasure give?
Pleasures only shadows be,
Cast by bodies we conceive,
And are made the things we deem
In those figures which they seem.

But these pleasures vanish fast
Which by shadows are exprest;
Pleasures are not if they last,
In their passage is their best:
Glory is most bright and gay
In a flash, and so away.

Feed apace then, greedy eyes,
On the wonder you behold;
Take it sudden as it flies,
Though you take it not to hold:
When your eyes have done their part,
Thought must length it in the heart.

EYES, HIDE MY LOVE.

EYES, hide my love, and do not show
    To any but to her my notes,
Who only doth that cipher know
    Wherewith we pass our secret thoughts:
Belie your looks in others' sight,
And wrong yourselves to do her right.

MICHAEL DRAYTON.

1563 1631.

TO HIS COY LOVE.

I PRAY thee, Love, love me no more,
　　Call home the heart you gave me;
I but in vain that saint adore,
　　That can, but will not save me:
These poor half kisses kill me quite;
　　Was ever man thus served?
Amidst an ocean of delight
　　For pleasure to be starved.

Show me no more those snowy breasts,
　　With azure rivers branched,
Where whilst my eye with plenty feasts,
　　Yet is my thirst not stanched.

Michael Drayton.

O Tantalus, thy pains ne'er tell,
    By me thou art prevented;
'T is nothing to be plagued in hell,
    But thus in heaven tormented!

Clip me no more in those dear arms,
    Nor thy life's comfort call me;
Oh, these are but too powerful charms,
    And do but more enthrall me.
But see how patient I am grown,
    In all this coyle about thee;
Come, nice thing, let thy heart alone, —
    I cannot live without thee.

LOVE BANISHED HEAVEN.

LOVE, banished heaven, in earth was held in scorn,
　　Wand'ring abroad in need and beggary;
And wanting friends, though of a goddess born,
Yet craved the alms of such as passèd by.
I, like a man devout and charitable,
Clothed the naked, lodged this wand'ring guest,
With sighs and tears still furnishing his table
With what might make the miserable blest.
But this ungrateful, for my good desert,
Enticed my thoughts against me to conspire,
Who gave consent to steal away my heart,
And set my breast, his lodging, on a fire.
　　Well, well, my friends, when beggars grow thus bold,
　　No marvel then though charity grow cold.

Michael Drayton.

DEFIANCE TO LOVE.

SHOOT, false Love! I care not:
   Spend thy shafts, and spare not!
I fear not, I, thy might,
And less I weigh thy spite;
All naked, I unarm me:
If thou canst, now shoot and harm me!
So lightly I esteem thee,
As now a child I deem thee.

Long thy bow did fear me,
While thy pomp did blear me:
But now I do perceive
Thy art is to deceive;
And every simple lover
All thy falsehood can discover.
Then weep, Love! and be sorry,
For thou hast lost thy glory.

THOMAS HEYWOOD.

—— ?-1649.

GREETINGS TO MY LOVE.

PACK clouds away, and welcome day;
    With night we banish sorrow;
Sweet air, blow soft; mount, larks, aloft,
    To give my love good-morrow!
Wings from the wind to please her mind,
    Notes from the lark, I'll borrow;
Bird, prune thy wing; nightingale, sing,
    To give my love good-morrow!
    To give my love good-morrow,
Notes from them all I 'll borrow.

Wake from thy nest, robin red-breast,
    Sing, birds, in every furrow,
And from each bill let music shrill
    Give my fair love good-morrow!
Blackbird and thrush, in every bush,
    Stare, linnet, and cock-sparrow,
You pretty elves, amongst yourselves,
    Sing my fair love good-morrow!
    To give my love good-morrow,
Sing, birds, in every furrow!

LOVE'S ECSTASY.

HENCE with passion, sighs, and tears,
    Disasters, sorrows, cares, and fears!
See, my Love, my Love appears,
    That thought himself exiled.
Whence might all these loud joys grow,
Whence might mirth and banquets flow,
But that he 's come, he 's come, I know?
    Fair Fortune, thou hast smiled.

Give [un]to these windows eyes,
Daze the stars and mock the skies,
And let us two, us two, devise
    To lavish our best treasures:
Crown our wishes with content,
Meet our souls in sweet consent,
And let this night, this night, be spent
    In all abundant pleasures.

TO PHYLLIS.

FROM "THE FAIR MAID OF THE EXCHANGE."

YE little birds that sit and sing
    Amidst the shady valleys,
And see how Phyllis sweetly walks
    Within her garden alleys;
Go, pretty birds, about her bower;
Sing, pretty birds, she may not lower:
Ah me! methinks I see her frown;
    Ye pretty wantons, warble.

Go, tell her through your chirping bills
    As you by me are bidden,
To her is only known my love
    Which from the world is hidden.
Go, pretty birds, and tell her so,
See that your notes strain not too low,
For still methinks I see her frown;
    Ye pretty wantons, warble.

Go, tune your voices' harmony,
    And sing I am her lover;
Strain loud and sweet, that every note
    With sweet content may move her.
And she that hath the sweetest voice,
Tell her I will not change my choice:
Yet still methinks I see her frown;
    Ye pretty wantons, warble.

Oh fly! make haste! see, see, she falls
    Into a pretty slumber;
Sing round about her rosy bed,
    That waking she may wonder;
Say to her 't is her lover true,
That sendeth love to you, to you;
And when you hear her kind reply,
    Return with pleasant warblings.

CHRISTOPHER MARLOWE.

THE PASSIONATE SHEPHERD TO HIS LOVE.

COME live with me and be my love,
    And we will all the pleasures prove
That hills and valleys, dales and fields,
Woods or steepy mountain yields.

And we will sit upon the rocks,
Seeing the shepherds feed their flocks,
By shallow rivers, to whose falls
Melodious birds sing madrigals.

And I will make thee beds of roses
And a thousand fragrant posies;
A cap of flowers, and a kirtle
Embroidered all with leaves of myrtle;

A gown made of the finest wool
Which from our pretty lambs we pull;
Fair linèd slippers for the cold,
With buckles of the purest gold;

A belt of straw and ivy buds,
With coral clasps and amber studs:
And if these pleasures may thee move,
Come live with me and be my love.

The shepherd swains shall dance and sing
For thy delight each May morning;
If these delights thy mind may move,
Come live with me and be my love.

WILLIAM SHAKESPEARE.

1564-1616.

TO SYLVIA.

FROM "TWO GENTLEMEN OF VERONA."

WHO is Sylvia? What is she
    That all our swains commend her?
Holy, fair, and wise is she;
    The heavens such grace did lend her
That she might admirèd be.

Is she kind as she is fair? —
    For beauty lives with kindness;
Love doth to her eyes repair
    To help him of his blindness;
And being helped, inhabits there.

Then to Sylvia let us sing,
 That Sylvia is excelling;
She excels each mortal thing
 Upon the dull earth dwelling;
To her let us garlands bring.

SONG.

FROM "LOVE'S LABOUR'S LOST."

ON a day (alack the day!)
    Love, whose month is ever May,
Spied a blossom passing fair
Playing in the wanton air;
Through the velvet leaves the wind,
All unseen, 'gan passage find,
That the lover, sick to death,
Wished himself the heaven's breath.
"Air," quoth he, "thy cheeks may blow;
Air, would I might triumph so!
But, alack, my hand is sworn
Ne'er to pluck thee from thy thorn:
Vow, alack, for youth unmeet,
Youth, so apt to pluck a sweet.
Do not call it sin in me
That I am forsworn for thee;
Thou, for whom Jove would swear
Juno but an Ethiop were,
And deny himself for Jove
Turning mortal for thy love."

TO IMOGEN.

FROM "CYMBELINE."

HARK, hark! the lark at heaven's gate sings,
    And Phœbus 'gins arise,
His steeds to water at those springs
    On chaliced flowers that lies;
And winking Mary-buds begin
    To ope their golden eyes:
With everything that pretty is,
        My lady sweet, arise;
            Arise, arise!

INCONSTANCY.

FROM "MUCH ADO ABOUT NOTHING."

SIGH no more, ladies, sigh no more, —
   Men were deceivers ever;
One foot in sea, and one on shore,
   To one thing constant never:
      Then sigh not so,
      But let them go,
  And be you blithe and bonny,
Converting all your sounds of woe
   Into hey nonny, nonny!

Sing no more ditties, sing no mo'
   Of dumps so dull and heavy;
The fraud of men was ever so
   Since summer first was leavy:
      Then sigh not so,
      But let them go,
  And be you blithe and bonny,
Converting all your sounds of woe
   Into hey nonny, nonny!

FANCY.

FROM "MERCHANT OF VENICE."

TELL me where is Fancy bred, —
In the heart or in the head?
How begot, how nourishèd?
Reply, reply.

It is engendered in the eyes,
With gazing fed; and Fancy dies
In the cradle where it lies.
Let us all ring Fancy's knell,
I'll begin it, — Ding, dong, bell,
Ding, dong, bell.

William Shakespeare.

THE RHYME OF WHITE AND RED.

FROM "LOVE'S LABOUR'S LOST."

IF she be made of white and red,
    Her faults will ne'er be known,
For blushing cheeks by faults are bred,
    And fears by pale white shown :
Then if she fear, or be to blame,
    By this you shall not know,
For still her cheeks possess the same,
    Which native she doth owe.

SPRING.

FROM "LOVE'S LABOUR'S LOST."

WHEN daisies pied, and violets blue,
    And lady-smocks all silver white,
And cuckoo-buds of yellow hue
    Do paint the meadows with delight,
The cuckoo then on every tree
Mocks married men; for thus sings he,
        "Cuckoo,
Cuckoo, cuckoo!" — Oh word of fear,
Unpleasing to a married ear!

When shepherds pipe on oaten straws,
    And merry larks are ploughman's clocks;
When turtles tread, and rooks and daws,
    And maidens bleach their summer smocks, —
The cuckoo then on every tree
Mocks married men; for thus sings he,
        "Cuckoo,
Cuckoo, cuckoo!" — Oh word of fear,
Unpleasing to the married ear!

BIRON'S CANZONET.

FROM "LOVE'S LABOUR'S LOST."

IF love make me forsworn, how shall I swear to
    love?
  Ah, never faith could hold, if not to beauty
    vowed!
Though to myself forsworn, to thee I 'll faithful
    prove;
  Those thoughts to me were oaks, to thee like
    osiers bowed.
Study his bias leaves, and makes his book thine
    eyes,
  Where all those pleasures live that art would
    comprehend.
If knowledge be the mark, to know thee shall
    suffice;
  Well learnèd is that tongue that well can thee
    commend,

73

All ignorant that soul that sees thee without wonder
    (Which is to me some praise, that I thy parts
        admire) ;
Thy eye Jove's lightning bears, thy voice his dread-
        ful thunder,
    Which, not to anger bent, is music and sweet
        fire.
Celestial as thou art, oh pardon love this wrong,
That sings Heaven's praise with such an earthly
        tongue !

William Shakespeare.

THE LOVER'S TEARS.

FROM "LOVE'S LABOUR'S LOST."

SO sweet a kiss the golden sun gives not
  To those fresh morning drops upon the rose,
As thy eye-beams, when their fresh rays have smote
  The night of dew that on my cheeks down flows;
Nor shines the silver moon one half so bright
  Through the transparent bosom of the deep,
As doth thy face through tears of mine give light.
  Thou shinest in every tear that I do weep;
No drop but as a coach doth carry thee,
  So ridest thou triumphing in my woe.
Do but behold the tears that swell in me,
  And they thy glory through my grief will show.
But do not love thyself; then thou wilt keep
My tears for glasses, and still make me weep.
O queen of queens, how far dost thou excel!
No thought can think, nor tongue of mortal tell.

PERJURY EXCUSED.

FROM "LOVE'S LABOUR'S LOST."

DID not the heavenly rhetoric of thine eye,
    'Gainst whom the world cannot hold argument,
Persuade my heart to this false perjury?
    Vows for thee broke deserve not punishment.
A woman I forswore; but I will prove,
    Thou being a goddess, I forswore not thee:
My vow was earthly, thou a heavenly love;
    Thy grace being gained cures all disgrace in me.
Vows are but breath, and breath a vapour is:
    Then thou, fair sun, which on my earth dost
        shine,
Exhalest this vapour-vow; in thee it is!
    If broken then, it is no fault of mine;
If by me broke, what fool is not so wise
To lose an oath to win a paradise?

OH, MISTRESS MINE.

FROM "TWELFTH NIGHT."

O MISTRESS mine, where are you roaming?
   Oh, stay and hear; your true love 's coming,
     That can sing both high and low.
Trip no farther, pretty sweeting;
Journeys end in lovers meeting,
     Every wise man's son doth know.

What is love? 't is not hereafter;
Present mirth hath present laughter;
     What 's to come is still unsure.
In delay there lies no plenty;
Then come kiss me, sweet-and-twenty,
     Youth 's a stuff will not endure.

IT WAS A LOVER AND HIS LASS.

FROM "TWELFTH NIGHT"

IT was a lover and his lass,
    With a hey and a ho and a hey nonino,
That o'er the green cornfield did pass
    In the spring-time, the only pretty ring-time,
When birds do sing, hey ding-a-ding, ding;
Sweet lovers love the spring.

Between the acres of the rye,
    With a hey and a ho and a hey nonino,
These pretty country-folks would lie,
    In the spring-time, the only pretty ring-time,
When birds do sing, hey ding-a-ding, ding;
Sweet lovers love the spring.

This carol they began that hour,
    With a hey and a ho and a hey nonino,
How that a life was but a flower
    In the spring-time, the only pretty ring-time,

When birds do sing, hey ding-a-ding, ding;
Sweet lovers love the spring.

And therefore take the present time
    With a hey and a ho and a hey nonino;
For love is crownèd with the prime
    In the spring-time, the only pretty ring-time,
When birds do sing, hey ding-a-ding, ding;
Sweet lovers love the spring.

SONG.

FROM "MEASURE FOR MEASURE."

TAKE, oh take those lips away
    That so sweetly were forsworn!
And those eyes, like break of day,
    Lights that do mislead the morn!
But my kisses bring again,
    Seals of love, but sealed in vain.

A BRIDAL SONG.

FROM THE "TWO NOBLE KINSMEN."

ROSES, their sharp spines being gone,
Not royal in their smells alone,
But in their hue;
Maiden pinks, of odour faint,
Daisies smell-less, yet most quaint,
And sweet thyme true;

Primrose, firstborn child of Ver,
Merry springtime's harbinger,
With her bells dim;
Oxlips in their cradles growing,
Marigolds on deathbeds blowing,
Larks'-heels trim.

All dear Nature's children sweet
Lie 'fore bride and bridegroom's feet,
Blessing their sense!

Not an angel of the air,
Bird melodious, or bird fair,
    Be absent hence !

The crow, the slanderous cuckoo, nor
The boding raven, nor chough hoar,
    Nor chattering pie,
May on our bride-house perch or sing,
Or with them any discord bring,
    But from it fly !

A WEDLOCK HYMN.

FROM "TWELFTH NIGHT."

WEDDING is great Juno's crown;
  Oh blessed bond of board and bed!
'T is Hymen peoples every town, —
  High wedlock then be honourèd:
Honour, high honour and renown,
  To Hymen, god of every town!

82

BEAUMONT AND FLETCHER.

1576-1625.

WEDDING SONG.

FROM "THE MAID'S TRAGEDY."

HOLD back thy hours, dark Night, till we have
    done !
    The day will come too soon ;
Young maids will curse thee if thou steal'st away
And leav'st their losses open to the day :
    Stay, stay, and hide
    The blushes of the bride !

Stay, gentle Night, and with thy darkness cover
    The kisses of her lover !
Stay, and confound her tears and her shrill cryings,
Her weak denials, vows, and often-dyings :
    Stay, and hide all ;
    But help not, though she call.

WAKE, GENTLY WAKE.

FROM "WIT AT SEVERAL WEAPONS."

FAIN would I wake you, sweet, but fear
    I should invite you to worse cheer;
In your dreams you cannot fare
Meaner than music, or compare;
None of your slumbers are compiled
Under the pleasures makes a child;
Your day-delights, so well compact
That what you think turns all to act,
I'd wish my life no better play
Your dream by night, your thought by day.
      Wake, gently wake,
    Part softly from your dreams;
      The morning flies
      To your fair eyes,
    To take her special beams.

SONG IN THE WOOD.

FROM "THE LITTLE FRENCH LAWYER."

THIS way, this way come, and hear,
  You that hold these pleasures dear;
Fill your ears with our sweet sound,
Whilst we melt the frozen ground.
This way come; make haste, O Fair!
Let your clear eyes gild the air;
Come, and bless us with your sight:
This way, this way, seek delight!

BRIDAL SONG.

FROM "THE LITTLE FRENCH LAWYER."

COME away! bring on the bride,
  And place her by her lover's side.
You fair troop of maids attend her;
Pure and holy thoughts befriend her.
Blush, and wish you virgins all
Many such fair nights may fall.
Hymen, fill the house with joy;
All thy sacred fires employ;
Bless the bed with holy love;
Now, fair orb of beauty, move!

JOHN FLETCHER.

1576-1625.

SPRING TIME AND LOVE.

FROM "VALENTINIAN."

I.

NOW the lusty spring is seen;
　　Golden yellow, gaudy blue,
　　Daintily invite the view;
Everywhere, on every green,
Roses, blushing as they blow,
　　And enticing men to pull;
Lilies, whiter than the snow;
　　Woodbines, of sweet honey full:
All love's emblems, and all cry,
　"Ladies, if not plucked, we die."

Yet the lusty spring has stayed;
    Blushing red, and purest white,
    Daintily to love invite
Every woman, every maid.
Cherries, kissing as they grow,
    And inviting men to taste;
Apples, even ripe below,
    Winding gently to the waist:
All love's emblems, and all cry,
"Ladies, if not plucked, we die."

II.

Hear, ye ladies that despise,
    What the mighty Love has done!
Fear examples, and be wise.
    Fair Caliston was a nun;
Leda, sailing on a stream,
    To deceive the hopes of man,
Love accounting but a dream,
    Doted on a silver swan;
Danaë, in a brazen tower,
Where no love was, loved a flower.

John Fletcher.

Hear, ye ladies that are coy,
  What the mighty Love can do!
Fear the fierceness of the boy,
  The chaste moon he makes to woo.
Vesta, kindling holy fires,
  Circled round about with spies,
Never dreaming loose desires,
  Doting, at the altar, dies.
Ilion in a short hour, higher
He can build, and once more fire.

TO MY MISTRESS'S EYES.

FROM "WOMEN PLEASED."

O FAIR sweet face! O eyes celestial bright!
  Twin stars in heaven, that now adorn the
    night!
O fruitful lips, where cherries ever grow!
And damask cheeks, where all sweet beauties blow!
O thou from head to foot divinely fair!
Cupid's most cunning net 's made of that hair,
And as he weaves himself for curious eyes,
"O me, O me! I 'm caught myself!" he cries:
Sweet rest about thee, sweet and golden sleep,
Soft peaceful thoughts your hourly watches keep,
Whilst I in wonder sing this sacrifice
To beauty sacred, and those angel eyes.

John Fletcher.

SERENADE.

FROM "THE SPANISH CURATE."

DEAREST, do not you delay me,
　　Since thou know'st I must be gone;
Wind and tide 't is thought doth stay me,
　　But 't is wind that must be blown
From that breath whose native smell
Indian odours doth excel.

Oh then speak, thou fairest fair,
　　Kill not him that vows to serve thee!
But perfume this neighbouring air,
　　Else dull silence sure will sterve me;
'T is a word that 's quickly spoken,
Which being restrained, a heart is broken.

TO ANGELINA.

FROM "THE ELDER BROTHER."

BEAUTY clear and fair
    Where the air
Rather like a perfume dwells,
    Where the violet and the rose
    Their blue veins and blush disclose,
And come to honour nothing else.

Where to live near,
    And planted there,
Is to live, and still live new;
    Where to gain a favour is
    More than light, perpetual bliss:
Make me live by serving you!

Dear, again back recall
    To this light
A stranger to himself and all;
    Both the wonder and the story
    Shall be yours, and eke the glory;
I am your servant and your thrall.

John Fletcher.

FROM "A WIFE FOR A MONTH."

LET those complain that feel Love's cruelty,
    And in sad legends write their woes;
With roses gently ' has corrected me,
    My war is without rage or blows:
My mistress's eyes shine fair on my desires,
And hope springs up inflamed with her new fires.

No more an exile will I dwell,
    With folded arms and sighs all day,
Reckoning the torments of my hell,
    And flinging my sweet joys away:
I am called home again to quiet peace;
My mistress smiles, and all my sorrows cease.

Yet what is living in her eye,
    Or being blessed with her sweet tongue,
If these no other joys imply?
    A golden gyve, a pleasing wrong!
To be your own but one poor month, I 'd give
My youth, my fortune, and then leave to live.

THOMAS DEKKER.

1570?-1641?

BEAUTY, ARISE!

FROM "THE PLEASANT COMEDY OF PATIENT GRISSELL."

BEAUTY, arise, show forth thy glorious shining!
   Thine eyes feed love, for them he standeth
      pining;
Honour and youth attend to do their duty
To thee, their only sovereign beauty.
Beauty, arise, whilst we, thy servants, sing
Io to Hymen, wedlock's jocund king!
   Io to Hymen, Io, Io, sing!
   Of wedlock, love, and youth is Hymen king.

Beauty, arise, thy glorious lights display!
Whilst we sing Io, glad to see this day.
   Io, Io, to Hymen, Io, Io, sing!
   Of wedlock, love, and youth is Hymen king.

Thomas Dekker.

THE INVITATION.

FROM "THE SUN'S DARLING."

LIVE with me still, and all the measures
    Played to by the spheres I 'll teach thee;
Let 's but thus dally, all the pleasures
    The moon beholds her man shall reach thee.

Dwell in mine arms, aloft we'll hover,
    And see fields of armies fighting :
Oh, part not from me ! I 'll discover
    There all but [?] books of fancy's writing.

Be but my darling, Age to free thee
    From her curse shall fall a-dying ;
Call me thy empress, Time to see thee
    Shall forget his art of flying.

THOMAS CAMPION.

1540 ?–1623 ?

LOVE'S REQUEST.

SHALL I come, sweet Love, to thee
    When the evening beams are set?
Shall I not excluded be,
    Will you find no feignèd let?
Let me not, for pity, more
Tell the long hours at your door!

Who can tell what thief or foe,
    In the covert of the night,
For his prey will work my woe,
    Or through wicked foul despite?
So may I die unredrest
Ere my long love be possest.

96

But to let such dangers pass,
    Which a lover's thoughts disdain,
'T is enough in such a place
    To attend love's joys in vain :
Do not mock me in thy bed,
While these cold nights freeze me dead.

TO LESBIA.

MY sweetest Lesbia, let us live and love;
    And though the sager sort our deeds reprove,
Let us not weigh them.   Heaven's great lamps do dive
Into their west, and straight again revive;
But soon as once set is our little light,
Then must we sleep one ever-during night.

If all would lead their lives in love like me,
Then bloody swords and armour should not be;
No drum nor trumpet peaceful sleeps should move,
Unless alarm came from the Camp of Love:
But fools do live and waste their little light,
And seek with pain their ever-during night.

When timely death my life and fortunes ends,
Let not my hearse be vext with mourning friends;
But let all lovers rich in triumph come,
And with sweet pastimes grace my happy tomb:
And, Lesbia, close up thou my little light,
And crown with love my ever-during night.

98

CHERRY RIPE.

THERE is a garden in her face
  Where roses and white lilies grow;
A heavenly paradise is that place
Wherein all pleasant fruits do flow:
    There cherries grow which none may buy,
    Till "Cherry ripe" themselves do cry.

Those cherries fairly do enclose
Of orient pearl a double row,
Which when her lovely laughter shows,
They look like rose-buds filled with snow;
    Yet them nor peer nor prince can buy,
    Till "Cherry ripe" themselves do cry.

Her eyes like angels watch them still,
Her brows like bended bows do stand,
Threatening with piercing frowns to kill
All that attempt with eye or hand
    Those sacred cherries to come nigh,
    Till "Cherry ripe" themselves do cry.

BEN JONSON.

SONG.

OH, do not wanton with those eyes,
    Lest I be sick with seeing;
Nor cast them down, but let them rise,
    Lest shame destroy their being.

Oh, be not angry with those fires,
    For then their threats will kill me;
Nor look too kind on my desires,
    For then my hopes will spill me.

Oh, do not steep them in thy tears,
    For so will sorrow slay me;
Nor spread them as distract with fears,
    Mine own enough betray me.

PERFECT BEAUTY.

FROM "THE NEW INN."

IT was a beauty that I saw,
    So pure, so perfect, as the frame
    Of all the universe was lame
To that one figure could I draw,
Or give least line of it a law!
    A skein of silk without a knot,
A fair march made without a halt,
A curious form without a fault,
    A printed book without a blot,
    All beauty, and without a spot!

THE TRIUMPH OF CHARIS.

FROM "THE DEVIL IS AN ASS."

SEE the chariot at hand here of Love,
    Wherein my lady rideth!
Each that draws is a swan or a dove,
    And well the car Love guideth.
As she goes, all hearts do duty
      Unto her beauty,
And enamoured do wish, so they might
      But enjoy such a sight,
That they still were to run by her side
Through swords, through seas, whither she would
    ride.

Do but look on her eyes; they do light
    All that Love's world compriseth!
Do but look on her hair; it is bright
    As Love's star, when it riseth!
Do but mark her forehead, smoother
      Than words that soothe her!

Ben Jonson.

And from her arched brows such a grace
      Sheds itself through the face
As alone there triumphs to the life,
All the gain, all the good, of the elements' strife !

Have you seen but a bright lily grow,
    Before rude hands have touched it?
Have you marked but the fall of the snow,
    Before the soil hath smutched it?
Have you felt the wool of the beaver,
      Or swan's down, ever?
Or have smelt o' the bud of the brier,
      Or the nard in the fire?
Or have tasted the bag of the bee?
Oh so white, oh so soft, oh so sweet is she !

TO CELIA.

DRINK to me only with thine eyes,
  And I will pledge with mine;
Or leave a kiss but in the cup,
  And I 'll not look for wine!
The thirst that from the soul doth rise
  Doth ask a drink divine,
But might I of Jove's nectar sup,
  I would not change for thine.

I sent thee late a rosy wreath,
  Not so much honoring thee
As giving it a hope that there
  It could not withered be;
But thou thereon did'st only breathe,
  And sent'st it back to me;
Since when it grows and smells, I swear,
  Not of itself, but thee.

THE SWEET NEGLECT.

FROM "THE SILENT WOMAN."

STILL to be neat, still to be drest
    As you were going to a feast;
Still to be powdered, still perfumed,
Lady, it is to be presumed,
Though art's hid causes are not found,
All is not sweet, all is not sound.

Give me a look, give me a face,
That makes simplicity a grace;
Robes loosely flowing, hair as free:
Such sweet neglect more taketh me
Than all the adulteries of art:
They strike mine eyes, but not my heart.

THE KISS.

FROM "CYNTHIA'S REVELS."

OH that joy so soon should waste !
  Or so sweet a bliss
  As a kiss
Might not forever last !
So sugared, so melting, so soft, so delicious !
  The dew that lies on roses
  When the morn herself discloses
Is not so precious.
Oh rather than I would it smother,
Were I to taste such another,
  It should be my wishing
  That I might die kissing !

Ben Jonson.

THE BANQUET OF SENSE.

FROM "THE POETASTER."

1. THEN in a free and lofty strain
       Our broken tunes we thus repair;
2. And we answer them again,
       Running division on the panting air:

Ambo.   To celebrate this feast of sense,
       As free from scandal as offence.

1.   Here is beauty for the eye;
2.   For the ear sweet melody;
1. Ambrosiac odours for the smell;
2.   Delicious nectar for the taste;

Ambo.   For the touch a lady's waist,
       Which doth all the rest excel.

TO A GLOVE.

FROM "CYNTHIA'S REVELS."

THOU more than most sweet glove
　　Unto my more sweet love:
Suffer me to store with kisses
This empty lodging, that now misses
The pure rosy hand that wear thee,
Whiter than the kid that bear thee.
Thou art soft, but that was softer;
Cupid's self has kissed it ofter
Than e'er he did his mother's doves,
Supposing her the queen of loves
That was thy mistress, best of gloves.

Ben Jonson.

VENETIAN SONG.

FROM "VOLPONE, OR THE FOX."

COME, my Celia, let us prove,
  While we can, the sports of love;
Time will not be ours forever,
He at length our good will sever.
Spend not then his gifts in vain:
Suns that set may rise again;
But if once we lose this light,
'T is with us perpetual night.
Why should we defer our joys?
Fame and rumour are but toys.
Cannot we delude the eyes
Of a few poor household spies?
Or his easier ears beguile,
Thus removèd by our wile?
'T is no sin love's fruits to steal;
But the sweet thefts to reveal,
To be taken, to be seen, —
These have crimes accounted been.

WILLIAM DRUMMOND.

1585–1649.

TO CHLORIS.

SEE, Chloris, how the clouds
   Tilt in the azure lists,
And how with Stygian mists
Each hornèd hill his giant forehead shrouds;
Jove thund'reth in the air;
The air, grown great with rain,
Now seems to bring Deucalion's days again.
I see thee quake; come, let us home repair;
Come, hide thee in mine arms,
If not for love, yet to shun greater harms.

MADRIGAL.

SWEET rose! whence is this hue
Which doth all hues excel?
Whence this most fragrant smell?
And whence this form and gracing grace in you?
In flowery Pœstum's field perhaps ye grew,
Or Hybla's hills you bred,
Or odoriferous Enna's plains you fed,
Or Tmolus, or where boar young Adon slew.
Or hath the Queen of Love you dyed of new
In that dear blood, which makes you look so red?
No! none of these, but cause more high you blissed:
My Lady's breast you bare, and lips you kissed.

SONG.

PHŒBUS, arise,
    And paint the sable skies
With azure, white, and red!
Rouse Memnon's mother from her Tithon's bed,
That she thy cáreer may with roses spread!
The nightingales thy coming each where sing
Make an eternal Spring,
Give life to this dark world which lieth dead.
Spread forth thy golden hair
In larger locks than thou wast wont before,
And, emperor like, decore
With diadem of pearls thy temples fair;
Chase hence the ugly night,
Which serves but to make dear thy glorious light!
This is that happy morn,
That day, long-wishèd day,
Of all my life so dark
(If cruel stars have not my ruin sworn,
And fates not hope betray),

Which, only white, deserves
A diamond forever should it mark :
This is the morn should bring unto this grove
My love, to hear and recompense my love.
Fair King, who all preserves,
But show thy blushing beams,
And thou two sweeter eyes
Shalt see than those which by Peneus' streams
Did once thy heart surprise ;
Nay, suns, which shine as clear
As thou when two thou did to Rome appear.
Now, Flora, deck thyself in fairest guise !
If that ye, Winds, would hear
A voice surpassing far Amphion's lyre,
Your stormy chiding stay ;
Let zephyr only breathe,
And with her tresses play,
Kissing sometimes these purple ports of death.
The winds all silent are,
And Phœbus in his chair,
Ensaffroning sea and air,
Makes vanish every star ;

Night like a drunkard reels
Beyond the hills to shun his flaming wheels !
The fields with flowers are decked in every hue,
The clouds bespangle with bright gold their blue ;
Here is the pleasant place,
And everything, save her, who all should grace.

GEORGE WITHER.

1588-1667.

SHALL I, WASTING IN DESPAIRE?

SHALL I, wasting in despaire,
Dye because a woman's fair!
Or make pale my cheeks with care
'Cause another's rosie are?
    Be she fairer than the day
    Or the flowry meads in May,
    If she thinke not well of me,
    What care I *how* faire she be?

Shall my seely heart be pined
'Cause I see a woman kind?

115

Or a well disposèd nature
Joynèd with a lovely feature?
    Be she meeker, kinder than
    Turtle-dove or Pelican, —
    If she be not so to me,
    What care I how kind she be?

Shall a woman's vertues move
Me to perish for her love?
Or her wel deservings knowne
Make me quite forget mine own?
    Be she with that goodness blest
    Which may merit name of best, —
    If she be not such to me,
    What care I how good she be?

'Cause her fortune seems too high
Shall I play the fool and die?
She that beares a noble mind,
If not outward helpes she find,
    Thinks what with them he wold do,
    That without them dares her woe:

And unlesse that minde I see,
What care I how great she be?

Great, or good, or kind, or faire,
I will ne'er the more despaire :
If she love me (this beleeve),
I will die ere she shall grieve.
 If she slight me when I woe,
 I can scorne and let her goe;
 For if she be not for me,
 What care I for whom she be?

A SONG TO HER BEAUTY.

FROM "THE MISTRESS OF PHILARETE."

AND her lips (that show no dulness)
   Full are, in the meanest fulness:
Those the leaves be whose unfolding
Brings sweet pleasures to beholding;
For such pearls they do disclose
Both the Indies match not those,
Yet are so in order placed
As their whiteness is more graced.
Each part is so well disposed,
And her dainty mouth composed,
So as there is no distortion
Misbeseems that sweet proportion.

    When her ivory teeth she buries
'Twixt her two enticing cherries,
There appear such pleasures hidden
As might tempt what were forbidden.

George Wither.

If you look again the whiles
She doth part those lips in smiles,
'T is as when a flash of light
Breaks from heaven to glad the night.

THOMAS CAREW.

1589-1639.

SONG.

WOULD you know what 's soft? I dare
    Not bring you to the down or air,
Nor to stars to show what 's bright,
Nor to snow to teach you white;

Nor, if you would music hear,
Call the orbs to take your ear;
Nor, to please your sense, bring forth
Bruisèd nard, or what 's more worth;

Or on food were your thoughts placed,
Bring you nectar for a taste.
Would you have all these in one, —
Name my mistress, and 't is done!

Thomas Carew.

A PRAYER TO THE WIND.

GO, thou gentle whispering wind,
    Bear this sigh; and if thou find
Where my cruel fair doth rest,
Cast it in her snowy breast:
So enflamed by my desire,
It may set her heart afire;
Those sweet kisses thou shalt gain
Will reward thee for thy pain.
Boldly light upon her lip,
There suck odours, and thence skip
To her bosom.   Lastly, fall
Down, and wander over all;
Range about those ivory hills
From whose every part distils
Amber dew; there spices grow,
There pure streams of nectar flow.
There perfume thyself, and bring
All those sweets upon thy wing.

As thou return'st, change by thy power
Every weed into a flower;
Turn each thistle to a vine,
Make the bramble eglantine.
For so rich a booty made,
Do but this, and I am paid.
Thou canst with thy powerful blast
Heat apace and cool as fast;
Thou canst kindle hidden flame,
And again destroy the same:
Then, for pity, either stir
Up the fire of love in her,
That alike both flames may shine,
Or else quite extinguish mine.

DISDAIN RETURNED.

HE that loves a rosy cheek,
    Or a coral lip admires,
Or from star-like eyes doth seek
    Fuel to maintain his fires, —
As Old Time makes these decay,
So his flames must waste away.

But a smooth and steadfast mind,
    Gentle thoughts and calm desires,
Hearts with equal love combined,
    Kindle never-dying fires :
Where these are not, I despise
Lovely cheeks or lips or eyes.

No tears, Celia, now shall win
    My resolved heart to return ;
I have searched thy soul within,
    And find nought but pride and scorn ;
I have learned thy arts, and now
Can disdain as much as thou !

THE PRIMROSE.

ASK me why I send you here
   This firstling of the infant year;
Ask me why I send to you
This primrose all bepearled with dew, —
I straight will whisper in your ears,
The sweets of love are washed with tears.

Ask me why this flower doth show
So yellow, green, and sickly too;
Ask me why the stalk is weak,
And bending, yet it doth not break, —
I must tell you, these discover
What doubts and fears are in a lover.

UNGRATEFUL BEAUTY.

KNOW, Celia, since thou art so proud,
   'T was I that gave thee thy renown.
Thou hadst in the forgotten crowd
   Of common beauties lived unknown,
Had not my verse exhaled thy name,
And with it impt the wings of Fame.

That killing power is none of thine, —
   I gave it to thy voice and eyes:
Thy sweets, thy graces, all are mine;
   Thou art my star, shin'st in my skies.
Then dart not from thy borrowed sphere
Lightning on him that fixed thee there.

Tempt me with such affrights no more,
   Lest what I made I uncreate;
Let fools thy mystic forms adore,
   I 'll know thee in thy mortal state.
Wise poets, that wrapt truth in tales,
Knew her themselves through all her veils.

CELIA SINGING.

YOU that think love can convey
    No other way
But through the eyes into the heart
    His fatal dart, —
Close up those casements, and but hear
    This siren sing;
    And on the wing
Of her sweet voice it shall appear
That love can enter at the ear.

Then unveil your eyes; behold
    The curious mould
Where that voice dwells: and as we know
    When the cocks crow
    We freely may
    Gaze on the day,
So may you, when the music 's done,
Awake and see the rising sun.

SONG.

ASK me no more where Jove bestows,
   When June is past, the fading rose;
For in your beauty's orient deep
These flowers, as in their causes, sleep.

Ask me no more whither do stray
The golden atoms of the day;
For, in pure love, Heaven did prepare
Those powders to enrich your hair.

Ask me no more whither doth haste
The nightingale, when May is past;
For in your sweet dividing throat
She winters, and keeps warm her note.

Ask me no more where those stars light
That downwards fall in dead of night;
For in your eyes they sit, and there
Fixèd become, as in their sphere.

Ask me no more if east or west
The phœnix builds her spicy nest;
For unto you at last she flies,
And in your fragrant bosom dies.

IN PRAISE OF HIS MISTRESS.

YOU that will a wonder know,
    Go with me:
Two suns in a heaven of snow
    Both burning be.
All they fire that do but eye them,
Yet the snow 's unmelted by them.

Leaves of crimson tulips met
    Guide the way
Where two pearly rows be set,
    As white as day;
When they part themselves asunder,
She breathes oracles of wonder.

All this but the casket is
    Which contains
Such a jewel, as to miss
    Breeds endless pains:
That 's her mind, and they that know it
May admire, but cannot show it.

RED AND WHITE ROSES.

READ in these roses the sad story
　　Of my hard fate and your own glory:
In the white you may discover
The paleness of a fainting lover;
In the red the flames still feeding
On my heart with fresh wounds bleeding.
The white will tell you how I languish,
And the red express my anguish;
The white my innocence displaying,
The red my martyrdom betraying.
The frowns that on your brow resided
Have those roses thus divided.
Oh, let your smiles but clear the weather,
And then they both shall grow together !

Thomas Carew.

THE PROTESTATION.

No more shall meads be decked with flowers,
  Nor sweetness dwell in rosy bowers,
Nor greenest buds on branches spring,
Nor warbling birds delight to sing,
Nor April violets paint the grove,
If I forsake my Celia's love.

The fish shall in the ocean burn,
And fountains sweet shall bitter turn;
The humble oak no flood shall know
When floods shall highest hills o'erflow;
Black Lethe shall oblivion leave, —
If e'er my Celia I deceive.

Love shall his bow and shaft lay by,
And Venus' doves want wings to fly;
The Sun refuse to show his light,
And day shall then be turned to night;
And in that night no star appear, —
If once I leave my Celia dear.

131

Love shall no more inhabit earth,
Nor lovers more shall love for worth,
Nor joy above in heaven dwell,
Nor pain torment poor souls in hell;
Grim death no more shall horrid prove, —
If e'er I leave bright Celia's love.

WILLIAM BROWNE.

1590–1645.

THE SIREN'S SONG.

FROM "A MASQUE OF THE INNER TEMPLE."

STEER, hither steer your wingèd pines,
    All beaten mariners !
Here lie Love's undiscovered mines,
    A prey to passengers ;
Perfumes far sweeter than the best,
Which make the Phœnix's urn and nest.
    Fear not your ships,
    Nor any to oppose you save our lips ;
But come on shore,
Where no joy dies till Love hath gotten more ;

For swelling waves our panting breasts,
    Where never storms arise,
Exchange, and be awhile our guests;
    For stars, gaze on our eyes!
The compass Love shall hourly sing,
And as he goes about the ring,
    We will not miss
    To tell each point he nameth with a kiss.
Then come on shore,
Where no joy dies till Love has gotten more.

SONG.

WELCOME, welcome do I sing,
   Far more welcome than the spring!
He that parteth from you never
   Shall enjoy a spring forever.

Love that to the voice is near,
   Breaking from your ivory pale,
Need not walk abroad to hear
   The delightful nightingale.
      Welcome, welcome then I sing,
         Far more welcome than the spring!
      He that parteth from you never
         Shall enjoy a spring forever.

Love, that looks still on your eyes
   Though the winter have begun
To benumb our arteries,
   Shall not want the summer's sun.
   Welcome, welcome, etc.

135

Love that still may see your cheeks,
  Where all rareness still reposes,
Is a fool if e'er he seeks
  Other lilies, other roses.
    Welcome, welcome, etc.

Love to whom your soft lip yields,
  And perceives your breath in kissing,
All the odours of the fields
  Never, never shall be missing.
    Welcome, welcome, etc.

Love that question would anew
  What fair Eden was of old,
Let him rightly study you,
  And a brief of that behold.
    Welcome, welcome, etc.

ROBERT HERRICK.

1591–1674.

THE ROCK OF RUBIES.

SOME asked me where the rubies grew;
    And nothing I did say,
But with my finger pointed to
    The lips of Julia.
Some asked how pearls did grow, and where;
    Then spoke I to my girl
To part her lips, and show me there
    The quarrelets of pearl.

137

UPON SAPPHO SWEETLY PLAYING AND SWEETLY SINGING.

WHEN thou dost play and sweetly sing,
    Whether it be the voice or string,
Or both of them, that do agree
Thus to entrance and ravish me, —
This, this I know, I 'm oft struck mute;
And die away upon thy lute.

TO MEADOWS.

YE have been fresh and green,
  Ye have been filled with flowers;
And ye the walks have been
  Where maids have spent their hours.

You have beheld how they
  With wicker arks did come,
To kiss and bear away
  The richer cowslips home.

You 've heard them sweetly sing,
  And seen them in a round, —
Each virgin, like a spring,
  With honeysuckles crowned.

But now we see none here
  Whose silvery feet did tread,
And with dishevelled hair
  Adorned this smoother mead.

Like unthrifts, having spent
   Your stock, and needy grown,
You 're left here to lament
   Your poor estates alone.

Robert Herrick.

DELIGHT IN DISORDER.

A SWEET disorder in the dress
    Kindles in clothes a wantonness:
A lawn about the shoulders thrown
Into a fine distraction;
An erring lace, which here and there
Enthrals the crimson stomacher;
A cuff neglectful, and thereby
Ribbons to flow confusedly;
A winning wave, deserving note,
In the tempestuous petticoat;
A careless shoe-string, in whose tie
I see a wild civility, —
Do more bewitch me, than when art
Is too precise in every part.

THE NIGHT PIECE.

HER eyes the glow-worm lend thee,
    The shooting stars attend thee;
        And the elves also,
        Whose little eyes glow
Like the sparks of fire, befriend thee.

No Will-o'-th'-Wisp mis-light thee;
Nor snake or slow-worm bite thee;
        But on, on thy way,
        Not making a stay!
Since ghost there's none to affright thee.

Let not the dark thee cumber;
What though the moon does slumber?
        The stars of the night
        Will lend thee their light,
Like tapers clear, without number.

Then, Julia, let me woo thee
Thus, thus to come unto me;
    And when I shall meet
    Thy silvery feet,
My soul I 'll pour into thee.

TO THE VIRGINS.

GATHER ye rosebuds while ye may,
  Old Time is still a-flying;
And this same flower that smiles to-day
  To-morrow will be dying.

The glorious lamp of heaven, the Sun,
  The higher he 's a-getting,
The sooner will his race be run,
  And nearer he 's to setting.

That age is best which is the first,
  When youth and blood are warmer;
But being spent, the worse and worst
  Times still succeed the former.

Then be not coy, but use your time,
  And while ye may, go marry;
For having lost but once your prime,
  You may forever tarry.

ART ABOVE NATURE.

WHEN I behold a forest spread
    With silken trees upon thy head;
And when I see that other dress
Of flowers set in comeliness;
When I behold another grace
In the ascent of curious lace,
Which like a pinnacle doth show
The top, and the top-gallant too;
Then when I see thy tresses bound
Into an oval, square or round,
And knit in knots far more than I
Can tell by tongue, or true-love tie;
Next, when those lawny films I see
Play with a wild civility;
And all those airy silks to flow,
Alluring me, and tempting so, —
I must confess, mine eye and heart
Dote less on nature than on art.

CHERRY-RIPE.

CHERRY-RIPE, ripe, ripe ! I cry,
　　Full and fair ones ; come and buy !
If so be you ask me where
They do grow? I answer, there
Where my Julia's lips do smile, —
There 's the land, or cherry-isle,
Whose plantations fully show
All the year where cherries grow.

TO THE ROSE.

GO, happy rose, and interwove
　　With other flowers, bind my love.
　　　Tell her, too, she must not be
　　　Longer flowing, longer free,
　　　That so oft has fettered me.

Say, if she 's fretful, I have bands
Of pearl and gold to bind her hands;
　　　Tell her, if she struggle still,
　　　I have myrtle rods at will
　　　For to tame, though not to kill.

Take thou my blessing thus, and go
And tell her this — But do not so!
　　　Lest a handsome anger fly
　　　Like a lightning from her eye,
　　　And burn thee up as well as I.

ON CHLORIS WALKING IN THE SNOW.

I SAW faire Chloris walke alone
  When feathered rain came softly down;
Then Jove descended from his Tower,
To court her in a silver shower.
The wanton snow flew to her breast,
Like little birds into their nest;
But overcome with whiteness there,
For griefe it thawed into a teare,
Then falling down her garment hem
To deck her, froze into a gem.

HOW ROSES CAME RED.

ROSES at first were white,
    Till they co'd not agree
Whether my Sappho's breast
    Or they more white sho'd be.

But being vanquisht quite,
    A blush their cheeks bespred;
Since which (beleeve the rest)
    The roses first came red.

JAMES SHIRLEY.

1594-1666.

THE LOOKING-GLASS.

WHEN this crystal shall present
    Your beauty to your eye,
Think! that lovely face was meant
    To dress another by.
For not to make them proud
These glasses are allowed
      To those are fair,
      But to compare
The inward beauty with the outward grace,
And make them fair in soul as well as face.

James Shirley.

A LULLABY.

FROM "THE TRIUMPH OF BEAUTY."

CEASE, warring thoughts, and let his brain
  No more discord entertain,
But be smooth and calm again.
Ye crystal rivers that are nigh,
As your streams are passing by
Teach your murmers harmony.
Ye winds that wait upon the Spring,
And perfumes to flowers do bring,
Let your amorous whispers here
Breathe soft music to his ear.
Ye warbling nightingales repair
From every wood to charm this air,
And with the wonders of your breast
Each striving to excel the rest, —
When it is time to wake him, close your parts
And drop down from the tree with broken hearts.

TO ONE SAYING SHE WAS OLD.

TELL me not Time hath played the thief
   Upon her beauty!   My belief
Might have been mocked, and I had been
An heretic, if I had not seen
My mistress is still fair to me.
And now I all those graces see
That did adorn her virgin brow:
Her eye hath the same flame in 't now
To kill or save; the chemist's fire
Equally burns, — so my desire;
Not any rose-bud less within
Her cheek; the same snow on her chin;
Her voice that heavenly music bears
First charmed my soul, and in my ears
Did leave it trembling; her lips are
The self-same lovely twins they were:
After so many years I miss
No flower in all my paradise.
Time, I despise thy rage and thee!
Thieves do not always thrive, I see.

ON HER DANCING.

I STOOD and saw my mistress dance,
    Silent, and with so fixed an eye
Some might suppose me in a trance.
    But being askèd why,
By one that knew I was in love,
    I could not but impart
My wonder to behold her move
So nimbly with a marble heart.

EDMUND WALLER.

1603-1686.

ON A GIRDLE.

THAT which her slender waist confined
　　Shall now my joyful temples bind;
No monarch but would give his crown
His arms might do what this has done!

It was my heaven's extremest sphere,
The pale which held that lovely deer!
My joy, my grief, my hope, my love,
Did all within this circle move!

A narrow compass, and yet there
Dwelt all that 's good and all that 's fair!
Give me but what this ribband bound,
Take all the rest the sun goes round!

TO CHLORIS.

WHILST I listen to thy voice,
    Chloris, I feel my heart decay;
That powerful voice
    Calls my fleeting soul away!
Oh, suppress that magic sound
Which destroys without a wound!

Peace, Chloris, peace! or singing die,
That together you and I
    To heaven may go:
    For all we know
Of what the blessed do above
Is that they sing, and that they love.

TO FLAVIA.

'TIS not your beauty can engage
    My wary heart:
The sun, in all his pride and rage,
    Has not that art!
And yet he shines as bright as you,
If brightness could our souls subdue.

'T is not the pretty things you say,
    Nor those you write,
Which can make Thyrsis' heart your prey:
    For that delight,
The graces of a well-taught mind,
In some of our own sex we find.

No, Flavia! 't is your love I fear;
    Love's surest darts,
Those which so seldom fail him, are
    Headed with hearts:
Their very shadows make us yield;
Dissemble well, and win the field!

STAY, PHŒBUS.

STAY, Phœbus ! stay !
  The world to which you fly so fast,
    Conveying day
From us to them, can pay your haste
With no such object, nor salute your rise
With no such wonder, as De Mornay's eyes.

Well does this prove
The error of those antique books
    Which made you move
About the world !   Her charming looks
Would fix your beams, and make it ever day,
Did not the rolling earth snatch her away.

SONG.

GO, lovely rose,
    Tell her that wastes her time and me,
That now she knows
When I resemble her to thee
How sweet and fair she seems to be.

Tell her that 's young,
And shuns to have her graces spied,
That had'st thou sprung
In deserts where no men abide,
Thou must have uncommended died.

Small is the worth
Of beauty from the light retired ;
Bid her come forth,
Suffer herself to be desired,
And not blush so to be admired.

Then die, that she
The common fate of all things rare
May read in thee, —
How small a part of time they share
Who are so wondrous sweet and fair !

WILLIAM HABINGTON.

1605-1645.

TO ROSES IN THE BOSOM OF CASTARA.

YE blushing virgins happy are
   In the chaste nunnery of her breasts,
For he 'd profane so chaste a fair
Who e'er should call them Cupid's nests.

Transplanted thus how bright ye grow,
How rich a perfume do ye yield!
In some close garden cowslips so
Are sweeter than i' th' open field.

William Habington.

In those white cloisters live secure
From the rude blasts of wanton breath,
Each hour more innocent and pure,
Till you shall wither into death.

Then that which living gave you room
Your glorious sepulchre shall be;
There wants no marble for a tomb,
Whose breast has marble been to me.

TO CUPID, UPON A DIMPLE IN
CASTARA'S CHEEK.

NIMBLE boy, in thy warm flight
    What cold tyrant dimmed thy sight?
Had'st thou eyes to see my fair,
Thou would'st sigh thyself to air
Fearing, to create this one,
Nature had herself undone.
But if you when this you hear
Fall down murdered through your ear,
Beg of Jove that you may have
In her cheek a dimpled grave.
Lily, rose, and violet
Shall the perfumed hearse beset;
While a beauteous sheet of lawn
O'er the wanton corpse is drawn;
And all lovers use this breath:
    "Here lies Cupid blest in death."

William Habington.

THE REWARD OF INNOCENT LOVE.

WE saw and wooed each other's eyes;
    My soul contracted then with thine,
And both burned in one sacrifice,
    By which the marriage grew divine.

Time 's ever ours while we despise
    The sensual idol of our clay;
For though the sun doth set and rise,
    We joy one everlasting day,

Whose light no jealous clouds obscure.
    While each of us shine innocent,
The troubled stream is still impure:
    With virtue flies away content.

And though opinion often err,
    We 'll court the modest smile of fame;
For sin's black danger circles her
    Who hath infection in her name.

Thus when to one dark, silent room
    Death shall our loving coffins thrust,
Fame will build columns on our tomb,
    And add a perfume to our dust.

SIR JOHN SUCKLING.

1609-1641.

ORSAMES' SONG.

FROM "AGLAURA."

WHY so pale and wan, fond lover?
  Prithee, why so pale?
Will, when looking well can't win her,
  Looking ill prevail?
  Prithee, why so pale?

Why so dull and mute, young sinner?
  Prithee, why so mute?
Will, when speaking well can't win her,
  Saying nothing do 't?
  Prithee, why so mute?

Quit, quit, for shame ! this will not move :
This cannot take her.
If of herself she will not love,
Nothing can make her :
The devil take her !

CONSTANCY.

OUT upon it! I have loved
    Three whole days together;
And am like to love three more,
    If it prove fair weather.

Time shall moult away his wings,
    Ere he shall discover
In the whole wide world again
    Such a constant lover!

But the spite on 't is, no praise
    Is due at all to me:
Love with me had made no stays
    Had it any been but she.

Had it any been but she,
    And that very face,
There had been at least ere this
    A dozen dozen in her place.

TRUE LOVE.

NO, no, fair heretic! it needs must be
  But an ill love in me,
  And worse for thee;
For were it in my power
To love thee now this hour
  More than I did the last,
'T would then so fall
  I might not love at all!
Love that can flow and can admit increase,
Admits as well an ebb, and may grow less.

True love is still the same; the torrid zones
  And those more frigid ones
  It must not know:
For love grown cold or hot
  Is lust, or friendship, not
  The thing we have.
For that 's a flame would die
Held down, or up too high.
Then think I love more than I can express,
And would love more, could I but love thee less.

Sir John Suckling.

SONG.

I PRITHEE send me back my heart,
    Since I can not have thine;
For if from yours you will not part,
    Why then shouldst thou have mine?

Yet now I think on 't, let it lie,
    To find it were in vain;
For th' hast a thief in either eye
    Would steal it back again!

Why should two hearts in one breast lie,
    And yet not lodge together?
O Love! where is thy sympathy,
    If thus our breasts thou sever?

But love is such a mystery,
    I cannot find it out;
For when I think I 'm best resolved,
    I then am in most doubt.

Then farewell care, and farewell woe,
  I will no longer pine;
For I 'll believe I have her heart
  As much as she hath mine.

RICHARD LOVELACE.

1618–1658.

TO ALTHEA FROM PRISON.

WHEN love with unconfinèd wings
    Hovers within my gates,
And my divine Althea brings
    To whisper at the grates;
When I lie tangled in her hair
    And fettered to her eye, —
The birds that wanton in the air
    Know no such liberty.

When flowing cups run swiftly round
    With no allaying Thames,
Our careless heads with roses bound,
    Our hearts with loyal flames;

When thirsty grief in wine we steep,
    When healths and draughts go free, —
Fishes that tipple in the deep
    Know no such liberty.

When, like committed linnets, I
    With shriller throat shall sing
The sweetness, mercy, majesty,
    And glories of my King;
When I shall voice aloud how good
    He is, how great should be, —
Enlargèd winds that curl the flood
    Know no such liberty.

Stone walls do not a prison make,
    Nor iron bars a cage;
Minds innocent and quiet take
    That for an hermitage;
If I have freedom in my love,
    And in my soul am free,
Angels alone, that soar above,
    Enjoy such liberty.

Richard Lovelace.

GOING TO THE WARS.

TELL me not, sweet, I am unkind,
    That from the nunnery
Of thy chaste breast and quiet mind
    To war and arms I fly !

True, a new mistress now I chase, —
    The first foe in the field ;
And with a stronger faith embrace
    A sword, a horse, a shield.

Yet this inconstancy is such
    As you too shall adore, —
I could not love thee, dear, so much,
    Loved I not honour more.

THE ROSE.

SWEET, serene, sky-like flower,
   Haste to adorn her bower!
      From thy long cloudy bed
      Shoot forth thy damask head!

New-startled blush of Flora,
The grief of pale Aurora
      (Who will contest no more),
      Haste, haste to strew her floor!

Vermilion ball that 's given
From lip to lip in heaven,
      Love's couch's coverled,
      Haste, haste to make her bed!

Dear offspring of pleased Venus
And jolly plump Silenus,
      Haste, haste to deck the hair
      O' the only sweetly fair!

174

See ! rosy is her bower;
Her floor is all this flower;
    Her bed a rosy nest
    By a bed of roses pressed !

ABRAHAM COWLEY.

1618-1667.

THE THIEF.

THOU robb'st my days of business and delights;
    Of sleep thou robb'st my nights.
Ah, lovely thief, what wilt thou do?
What, rob me of heaven too?
Thou even my prayers dost steal from me,
And I, with wild idolatry,
Begin to God, and end them all to thee!

Is it a sin to love, that it should thus
Like an ill conscience torture us?
Whate'er I do, where'er I go
(None guiltless e'er was haunted so),

176

Still, still, methinks thy face I view,
And still thy shape does me pursue,
As not you me, but *I* had murdered you.

From books I strive some remedy to take,
But thy name all the letters make
Whate'er 't is writ; I find *that* there,
Like points and commas, everywhere.
Me blest for this let no man hold;
For I, as Midas did of old,
Perish by turning everything to gold.

LOVE IN HER SUNNY EYES.

LOVE in her sunny eyes does basking play;
 Love walks the pleasant mazes of her hair;
Love does on both her lips forever stray,
And sows and reaps a thousand kisses there:
In all her outward parts Love 's always seen:
But, oh! he never went within.